GUIDE TO
FRANCE

W9-AWK-780

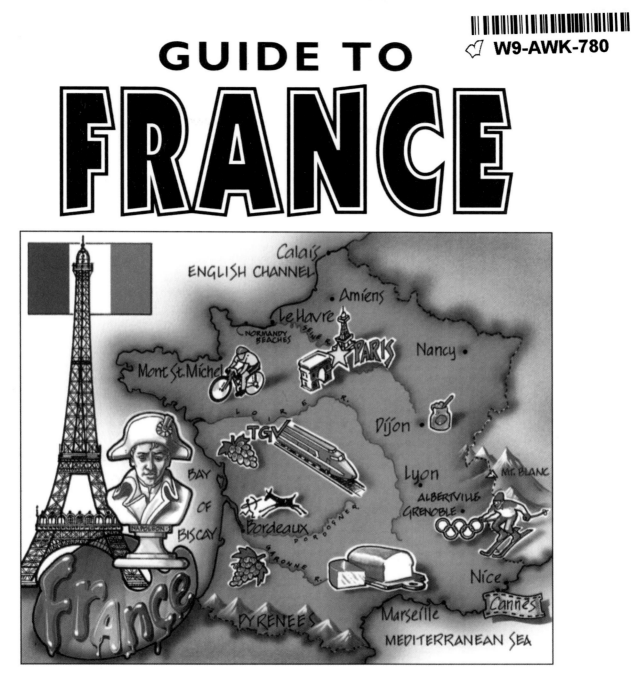

MICHAEL MARCH

Highlights for Children

CONTENTS

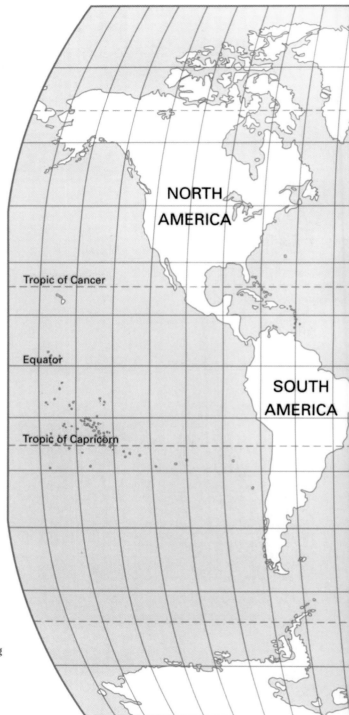

On the cover: The busy Avenue des Champs Elysées in the center of Paris with the famous Arc de Triomphe in the background.

The publisher is grateful for the guidance of Kevin McGeough, a Ph.D. candidate in ancient Near Eastern archaeology and languages at the University of Pennsylvania. He holds a master's degree in ancient Near Eastern archaeology and early modern European history and is currently teaching at the University of Lethbridge in Canada.

Published by Highlights for Children
©1995 Highlights for Children, Inc.
P.O. Box 18201
Columbus, OH 43218-0201
For information on *Top Secret Adventures,* visit
www.tsadventures.com or call 1-800-962-3661.

All rights reserved. No part of this book may be reproduced or transmitted in any form or by any means, electronic or mechanical, including photocopying, recording, or by any information storage and retrieval system, without permission in writing from the publisher.

18 17 16 15
ISBN 978-0-87534-913-8

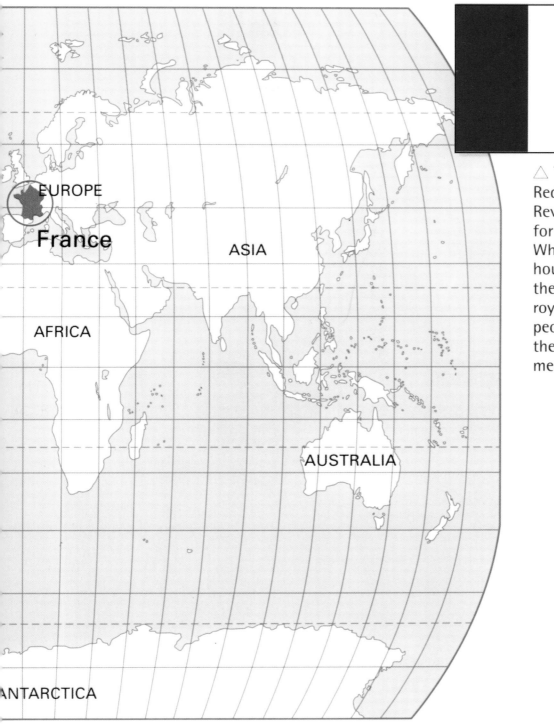

EUROPE

France

ASIA

AFRICA

AUSTRALIA

ANTARCTICA

△ **The French flag**
Red stands for the
Revolution and blue
for the capital, Paris.
White is for the
house of Bourbon,
the former French
royal family. French
people call their flag
the *tricolore*, which
means three colors.

3

FRANCE AT A GLANCE

Area 211,207 square miles (547,026 square kilometers)

Population 64,057,792

Capital Paris, population 2,187,534

Other big cities Lyon (489,005), Marseille (779,679), Toulouse (458,600), Nice (331,397)

Highest mountain Mont Blanc, 15,770 feet (4,807 meters)

Longest river Loire, 630 miles (1,020 kilometers)

Largest lake Lac Léman (Lake Geneva), 225 square miles (580 square kilometers)—most of it is in Switzerland; Lac d'Annecy is the largest within France, 10 square miles (27 square kilometers)

Official language French

▽ **French postage stamps** Two show the Eiffel Tower and the city of Marseille. Others depict famous people and French cuisine.

◁ **French money** The currency of France is the euro (€). The country belongs to the European Union (EU) and has the same currency as other EU member countries. For example, this 10-euro note could be used in Germany or Ireland.

© Oxford Cartographers

WALES

ENGLAND

NETHERLANDS

BELGIUM

FRANCE

Farmland &
Woodland
Mountains

★ Capital
● Major Cities
▲ Mountain Peaks
── Country Boundary

0   25   50 Miles
0   50   100 Kilometers

Strait of Dover

Calais

5°W

English Channel

50°N

LUXEMBOURG

GERMANY

Le Havre

Reims

Caen

CALVADOS

Seine

Strasbourg

Brest

N O R M A N D Y

Paris
★
Versailles

*A
L
S
A
C
E*

LIECHT.

B R I T T A N Y

Chartres

Le Mans

Troyes

Orléans

SWITZERLAND

Loire

Nantes

Tours

Dijon

*Lac
Léman*

P

La Rochelle

Y

Lyon

Mont Blanc

R

Cognac

▲

ITALY

45°N

Bay of

DORDOGNE

Massif

Grenoble

E

Biscay

Bordeaux

*A
U
V
E
R
G
N
E*

Central

Rhône

N

*L
A
N
D
E
S*

Albi

Avignon

PROVENCE

Nîmes

Nice

MONACO

Arles

Cannes

Monte-Carlo

Toulouse

Camargue

St.
Tropez

Marseille

Côte d' Azur

N

Lourdes

W   E

S

P y r é n é e s

Carcassonne

*Golfe du
Lion*

CORSICA
(France)

ANDORRA

S   P   A   I   N

0°

5°E

M e d i t e r r a n e a n

Sea

5

EUROPE'S HEXAGON

France is the second largest country in Europe, after Ukraine. It stretches from the English Channel in the north to the Mediterranean Sea and Spain in the south. The French often call their country *l'hexagone*, or the hexagon. On the map the shape of the country looks as if it has six sides.

Most of France's borders are natural landmarks. Sea or mountains close the country in on five of its six sides. Northern and western France are mostly fertile plains, where farmers expect rain all year round. People in the south enjoy hot, dry summers with lots of sunshine. But winter brings the *mistral*, a fierce chilly wind that can blow down the Rhône Valley for many days without stopping. Farther inland, winters are much colder, with heavy snows in the mountains.

▽ **A French food store** There are delicious cheeses and wines. *Saucissons*, spicy sausages, hang above the counter.

The Eiffel Tower, Paris

This world-famous landmark was erected by Gustave Alexandre Eiffel for the Paris Exposition of 1889.

Green fields in Normandy

This region is one of the best farming areas in France. The famous Camembert cheese is made here.

France is a land of wonderful scenery. It has a proud history and many lovely old buildings. France has given the world many famous artists, writers, musicians, clothes designers, and movie makers. It is also known for its fine wines and good food.

The official language is French, but other languages are spoken here, too. The Basques, who live near the border with Spain, speak their own language. So do the Bretons of the northwest. The Moroccans, Vietnamese, and other people from abroad have brought their own language and culture to France.

As a visitor here, you can share the excitement of riding on one of the world's fastest passenger trains. The TGVs, or *Trains à Grande Vitesse,* run between most major cities. Or you can travel by car on some of the best roads in Europe.

THE BEAUTIFUL CAPITAL

Paris, the capital of France, is one of the world's best-loved old cities. For hundreds of years, artists, poets, and tourists have come to Paris. Stroll along the banks of the Seine River, or mix with the Parisiens at a bustling outdoor café — these are both good ways to get to know the city's charm.

The oldest district of Paris is the Île de la Cité, an island in the middle of the Seine. Here you will find the great cathedral Notre Dame de Paris, completed in the year 1200. Outside, it looks grand and dark. Inside, light streams through its beautiful stained-glass windows. The island's old prison, the Conciergerie, is truly grim. Marie-Antoinette, the queen who was beheaded in the French Revolution, was held here as a prisoner. You can visit her tiny cell.

A boat trip down the Seine will show you more of the city. The enormous Louvre Museum houses some of the world's greatest art treasures. Two of the most famous are the *Venus de Milo*, the ancient Greek statue with broken arms, and the painting of *Mona Lisa* by Leonardo da Vinci. The tomb of the great French emperor, Napoleon Bonaparte, is on the opposite bank of the river in Les Invalides. Ahead, the Eiffel Tower rises 1,050 feet (320 meters) above the city.

You can explore the center of Paris on foot or ride the Métro (subway). The Boulevard Haussmann, with its many boutiques and department stores, is one of the best-known shopping streets in Paris. But if you are bargain hunting, you should try the Marché aux Puces. This famous fleamarket is in the northern part of the city.

Some Paris restaurants are very expensive, but others are quite reasonable. Whichever you choose, eating out in Paris is another of the city's delights.

▷ **The glass pyramid and the Louvre** The pyramid that forms the entrance to the museum is made of 675 panes of glass.

▽ **A Paris Métro station** *Le Métro* is the subway system that runs under the streets of France's capital.

▽ **The Galeries Lafayette department store** This famous shoppers' paradise is in the center of Paris.

ART AND REVOLUTION

The church Basilique du Sacré Coeur is in the district of Montmartre in northern Paris. It stands on a steep hill and overlooks the center of the city. At night its white domes are lit up brilliantly against the sky. In the 1890s, famous painters gathered in this district. Some of them used to visit the famous old theater Moulin Rouge, which is nearby. Artists still work in Montmartre.

▷ **On the banks of the Seine** Here you can find paintings, drawings, and prints for sale. You can also buy books and picture postcards. The shops are called *bouquinistes*.

▽ **The Place de la Concorde** In this square stands a 3,200-year-old obelisk, or stone pillar, brought from Egypt in 1833.

Young people and students gather in Paris's lively Latin Quarter, on the left bank of the Seine. Its streets are lined with cafés, used bookstores, and art galleries. Since the 1700s, writers, artists, musicians, and even political rebels have met here. One café has a hat on display that Napoleon is said to have left behind. The heart of the Latin Quarter is the Sorbonne. It is the oldest university in France and one of the oldest in Europe.

The Bastille was a grim prison fortress that once stood in the Place de la Bastille. On July 14, 1789, the poor people of Paris rose up and stormed the fortress. This was the start of the French Revolution that led to the downfall of the kings and queens of France. Today France is a republic, with a president, not a monarch, as its head of state. You can visit the magnificent Palais de Versailles, just outside Paris, where the French royal family once lived in luxury.

From the presidential building, in the center of Paris, you can walk down the broad Avenue des Champs Elysées. At one end is the Arc de Triomphe. Napoleon had this huge monument built to honor his army. Beyond it, westward, is the Grande Arche. This equally big arch was built in the 1980s. It is a good example of modern architecture.

◁ **The Place du Tertre, behind the Sacré Coeur** In summer the square fills with artists and tourists, and the sidewalk cafés are busy.

11

GOING SOUTH

From Paris, the high-speed train called the TGV take a couple of hours to reach Lyon. Even traveling at speeds of over 180 miles (300 kilometers) per hour, you can be sure of a smooth, comfortable ride. The rolling hills, forests, and vineyards of the region of Burgundy flash by the window. You pass through countryside where winegrowers produce some of the finest wines in the world.

Lyon lies in the Rhône Valley and is one of France's major cities. For a long time Lyon has been known for producing silk and cloth. Today you will also see chemical and steel factories here. Lyon is an old city, with a history that began before the Romans invaded France in 58 B.C.

A huge granite plateau rises on the west side of the Rhône Valley. This is the Massif Central, a mountainous area where the scenery is wild but beautiful. Sheep and cattle graze on the high ground. Farmers grow corn and tobacco in the lowlands. The Auvergne region of the Massif is known for its cheeses. This region is also famous for its traditional songs and dances, such as the *bourrée*, an ancient kind of waltz.

To the southeast of Lyon, the city of Grenoble nestles in the foothills of the Alps, a vast mountain range. Some of the pretty Alpine villages nearby have grown into popular ski resorts. At 15,571 feet (4,807 meters), Mont Blanc, near the border with Italy, is Europe's highest mountain. You can take a cable car almost to the top. From there enjoy a wonderful view of mountain glaciers and the valley far below. Farther north, close to the Swiss border, lies the town of Evian. It is famous for its clear and fresh spring water.

▷ **The old Château de Polignac, near the town of Le Puy in the Massif Central** A *puy* is a rocky lava peak left over from an ancient volcano.

▷ **Schoolchildren on an Alpine skiing trip** The first Winter Olympic Games were held at the small village of Chamonix, below Mont Blanc, in 1924.

▷ **The mountain city of Grenoble** At one time the city was best known for its glove factories and its fine walnuts. Now Grenoble is an important industrial center.

THE "SKY-BLUE COAST"

The French Alps sweep down to the shores of the Mediterranean Sea. The famous Côte d'Azur, or Azure Coast, lies between the mountains and the sea. St. Tropez, Cannes, and Nice are favorite coastal resorts. Many tourists, including movie stars and other famous people, vacation here. They come to enjoy the fine weather and the sea. Painters love the clear light and bright colors of the Côte d'Azur.

In the hills overlooking the coast, you can explore some lovely old villages. Many of them have steep, narrow, cobblestone streets. There may be a fountain splashing in a shaded little courtyard. Some of these villages were carved out of local stone hundreds of years ago. They were built high up on cliff tops to stop attacks by bandits.

If you follow the hilly coast road from Nice toward the Italian border, you will come to Monaco. This tiny country is smaller than New York's Central Park. Monaco is ruled by a prince, but is protected by France. Many of the people you meet here are French. The Monte Carlo district is famous for its casinos and for the international car race, the Grand Prix de Monaco, that takes place here.

The beautiful island of Corsica lies about 100 miles (180 kilometers) out to sea.

▷ **People relaxing at Les Calanques, near Marseille** The name comes from an old local word *calanco*, meaning "steep cliff."

Snow-capped mountains, thick forests, deep gorges, and sandy beaches fringed with palm trees fill the wild landscape. Corsica became part of France in 1769. In that same year, Napoleon Bonaparte, the most famous of all Corsicans, was born. But Napoleon fought against Corsica's freedom, and he is no hero to the Corsicans.

◁ **On the road to Nice and Monaco** The blue signs are for expressways, where drivers pay *péage*, a toll. Genoa (Gênes in French) lies across the Italian border two hours' drive from Nice. Roquebrune is a pretty hilltop village.

▽ **The coastal town of Menton** With the warmest weather on the Côte d'Azur, Menton is a year-round resort. There are fine beaches, lemon trees, and a lovely old town district perched above the harbor.

HISTORIC CITIES

Marseille, on the Côte d'Azur, is the oldest city in France. It was founded more than 2,600 years ago, perhaps by the Greeks or the Phoenicians. Today, Marseille is the busiest port in France and the biggest city anywhere on the Mediterranean coast.

Marseille has a long and proud tradition of shipbuilding. Modern industries have now grown here, too. There are steelworks, oil refineries, and all kinds of factories. The city has two harbors. The Old Harbor has been used since the times of the Greeks. But now you will find mostly fishing boats anchored along the docks here. Larger ships use the Modern Harbor, which is much deeper.

During the French Revolution, soldiers from Marseille marched to Paris. On the way they sang the "Marseillaise" (Woman of Marseille), the rousing song that is now the national anthem of France.

Avignon, to the northwest, also has a rich history. It has a ruined 12th-century bridge and two 14th-century palaces. The popes, the leaders of what is now known as the Roman Catholic Church, used these palaces, when in France, from 1340 to 1791.

◁ **A festival at Arles** Riders in traditional costume gather outside the arena. This great oval amphitheater was built by the Romans more than 2,000 years ago.

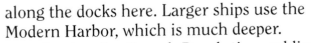

▷ **The Pont du Gard, near Nîmes** The beautiful Roman aqueduct was built about 19 B.C. to carry water across the Gard valley to the city of Nîmes. It is 900 feet (275 meters) long and 160 feet (49 meters) high.

The grape harvest There are vineyards all along the Mediterranean coast, from Cannes in the east to the Spanish border in the west.

Avignon lies on the Rhône River above the Rhône Delta. Here, the river splits into two channels before flowing into the sea. Between the two channels is the Camargue. This beautiful nature park is covered with marshland and lagoons. Flamingoes, black bulls, beavers, and wild gray horses all live here. Some of the wild gray horses of the Camargue are rounded up by the local people who sell rides to visitors. A few of the bulls end up in the bullrings of Arles and Nîmes. These two ancient cities have Roman arenas where bullfights are held.

THE PYRENEES

The city of Toulouse lies about 60 miles (100 kilometers) north of the border. The rugged Pyrenees mountains form the border between France and Spain. The mountains stretch from the Mediterranean Sea to the Atlantic Ocean. Toulouse has been called the pink city because the houses in the city's old quarter are built of reddish-pink brick. Many of these fine old buildings have stood for hundreds of years.

But Toulouse is also a modern city. It is the center of France's aerospace industry. European Airbus passenger airplanes are made here. A huge new hall for airplane assembly has been built.

The artist Henri de Toulouse-Lautrec came from this region. The house where he was born is in the little town of Albi, to the northeast of Toulouse. The most complete collection of Lautrec's paintings is in Albi.

Before the 13th century, Toulouse was the capital of a region that was independent of France. The local people even had their own language. But they were conquered by the kings of France. Many people died in the fighting or were murdered. The last place to resist was the mountain fortress of Montségur. It finally fell in 1244, fifteen years after Toulouse was captured. You can visit the ruins of Montségur in the foothills of the Pyrenees.

The region's most impressive sight is the medieval city of Carcassonne. With its pointed towers and high stone walls it looks like a storybook castle. On the way from Toulouse to Carcassonne, you can stop at Castelnaudary to try the famous *cassoulet*. This rich stew is made with white beans, pork, goose fat, and spicy sausage.

◁ **Playing boules** This popular ball game is played in almost every town and village in the south of France. It is also called *pétanque*.

▷ **The count's castle at Carcassonne** The Romans began to build the city 2,000 years ago. Most of the present walls and towers date back to the 12th and 13th centuries.

▷ **The holy town of Lourdes** People from all over the world come here to pray to Sainte Bernardette for a miracle cure. The town is in the northern Pyrenees Mountains, near the border between France and Spain.

UP THE ATLANTIC COAST

The people of the western Pyrenees, near the Atlantic coast, are Basques. Many more Basques live across the border in Spain. They are a proud people, with their own language, which some of them still speak. They have their own traditions and even their own red, white, and green flag.

▷ **Catching up on the news in Périgord** The man is wearing a *béret*, a soft, flat cap.

▽ **The lovely Old Harbor at La Rochelle** The towers standing at the entrance to the town from the Atlantic Ocean are 600 years old.

▽ **The Basque resort of Biarritz** Good surfing, sandy beaches, salty springs, excellent hotels, and a mild climate have helped make Biarritz a world-famous resort.

Most of the Basques in France are farmers. They grow corn and raise sheep, cattle, and horses. The local horse fairs draw big crowds. You can spot Basque men by their black bérets, a soft, flat hat.

Even the smallest Basque village has a court for *pelote*, their national game. Pelote is like squash. The ball is hit with a wicker basket tied to the wrist, instead of a racket. At festival times, Basque folk dances are exciting to watch. High acrobatic jumps and whooping cries are all part of the act. Basque shepherds use these cries to call to each other across the valleys.

The Landes is western Europe's biggest pine forest. It stands on the edge of one of the most famous wine-growing regions in France. The center of the region is the town of Bordeaux. The ancient Romans were the first people to grow grapes and make wine in Bordeaux. By the Middle Ages, the local people were producing more wine than they needed for themselves, so they began to sell some to England.

Truffles are a famous delicacy of the Périgord region. Using their keen sense of smell, dogs and pigs are traditionally used to discover these underground mushrooms.

Farther inland, in the Lascaux Cave there are pictures that are more than 17,000 years old. Bulls, deer, and other animals are painted in yellow, red, black, and brown on the cave walls. The paintings were found in 1940 by boys looking for their lost dog.

CASTLES AND KINGS

History is all around you in the Loire Valley. Here the French kings built hundreds of *châteaux*. These castlelike homes stood on the banks of the Loire River and alongside smaller rivers nearby. The earliest of these, such as the castle at Chinon, were built to be fortresses in times of war. Other châteaux were built and luxuriously furnished in peacetime as beautiful places fit for a king. You can still see them by the Loire today.

Chinon castle is now in ruins, but it is well worth a visit. It was there, in 1429, that France's greatest heroine, Joan of Arc, asked the French king to give her an army. She wanted to drive the English out of France. Two months later, she defeated the English in battle at the city of Orléans. Joan of Arc was captured and executed by the English. But every year in May the people of Orléans still celebrate her victory.

△ **Prizegiving at Le Mans** The famous 24-hour car race is held here every year.

◁ **The Futuroscope park** Located outside the ancient town of Poitiers, the park is a gigantic museum of modern movie film technology.

From Orléans, the Loire River winds westward across the plain toward the port of Nantes and the Atlantic Ocean, more than 600 miles (1,000 kilometers) away from its spring in the Massif Central.

In the middle of the fertile Loire Valley is the town of Tours. Grapes, asparagus, and strawberries grow here. Tours is also known as the town where the purest form of the French language is spoken. One of France's greatest writers, Honoré de Balzac, was born in Tours in 1799. There is a museum nearby showing many objects and works from his life. Another great writer, François Rabelais, came from near Chinon. Rabelais lived three hundred years earlier than Balzac. You can still visit the house where he was born.

The town of Chartres, in the wheat-growing region to the northeast, has one of France's finest cathedrals.

◁ **Château de Chambord, Loire Valley** Chambord is by far the biggest of the Loire châteaux. Inside there are 440 rooms and eighty-five staircases. The Château stands in a deer park and was built on the orders of François I as his vacation and hunting lodge.

BRETONS AND NORMANS

The westernmost region of France is called Bretagne (Brittany). It juts out into the sea north of where the Loire River ends. The Atlantic waves crash against the cliffs, but the sandy beaches offer good swimming.

Brittany is named after the people from the British Isles who settled here 1,500 years ago. The present-day Bretons (people of Brittany) are their descendants. The Breton language is quite unlike French. Although still spoken, the Breton language is slowly dying out. Many places in the Breton region do not have French names.

Bretons are great sailors, and much of the local cooking uses fish, as in *cotriade*, a rich stew. But today, farming is even more important. Half of all France's eggs are laid by Breton hens. Eggs are main ingredients in *crêpes*, or pancakes, a speciality of Brittany.

To the northeast of Brittany lies the rich farming land of Normandy. This region is named after the Normans, who came here from Scandinavia more than 1,000 years ago. Fine cheeses are produced here. Normandy was also the site of a famous battle during World War II. In 1944, soldiers from the United States, Great Britain, and other countries landed here to regain the area from German forces. Some beaches on the Normandy coast have American names, such as Omaha and Utah. Nearby, the town of Deauville is well known as a summer resort. The racecourse at Deauville is also famous.

The busy port of Le Havre, located at the mouth of the Seine River, is the second-biggest port in France. Farther up the Seine lies Rouen, the ancient capital of the region. It was here, on the old market square, that English soldiers burned Joan of Arc at the stake in 1431. They had declared that she was a witch.

▽ **On a traffic circle in Rouen is a statue of Napoleon** Rouen is France's largest river port and a center of its cotton industry.

◁ **Breton women in traditional costume**
It is festival time, and the women are wearing headdresses made from Breton lace.

▽ **The abbey of Mont Saint-Michel, Normandy** This is one of France's most popular tourist sites. You can walk to the little island from the mainland at low tide.

OLD ENEMIES, NEW FRIENDS

An undersea tunnel connects the French port of Calais with England. Today, the French and British people are friends. Both countries are members of the European Union. Prior to the mid 1800s they were often at war. In the center of Calais stands a bronze statue by the great French sculptor Auguste Rodin. It honors six "Burghers of Calais." In 1348, these citizens offered to lay down their lives if the invading English armies would spare the town.

The huge graveyards of Flanders and in Picardy tell the story of a much more recent conflict. Here, thousands of soldiers lie buried. They died during World War I (1914-1918). This time, the French and British fought together against the Germans.

The northern plain used to be France's industrial heartland. But less coal and steel is produced here today. As you move east, the land becomes hillier. The grapes grown on the chalky slopes of the Marne Valley are used for making champagne. Nearby, in the city of Reims, you can visit one of the greatest cathedrals in Europe. For 800 years, the kings of France were crowned here.

△ **A World War I cemetery in northern France** Much of the most severe fighting of the war took place in this region.

Farther east, the neat villages of Alsace, with their half-timbered houses, look more German than French. In fact, the Alsace region on the German border and Lorraine to the west have been ruled by Germany in the past.

But today Strasbourg, the Alsatian capital, is a sign of French and German friendship. Strasbourg is also the home of the European Parliament. A visit to this fine old city on the Rhine River marks the end of your journey through one of the most beautiful countries in Europe.

△ **A town in the Ardennes** The old town hall is made of red sandstone brick. The Ardennes region, near Belgium, suffered badly from flooding when the Meuse River overflowed its banks early in 1995.

◁ **Strasbourg, capital of Alsace** The spire of the cathedral rises above the town. From the top of the cathedral tower you get a wonderful view of the city. You can also see into the Black Forest in Germany to the east of Strasbourg.

FRANCE FACTS AND FIGURES

People

France has always been a popular country for immigrants. In Roman times, tribes from central Europe called Gauls and German tribes called Franks settled in France. The Romans conquered it and settled there. Scandinavians moved to Normandy at a later time. Even today, people from all over the world move to France, especially from Southeast Asia, North Africa, and the Caribbean.

Trade and Industry

France is one of the world's greatest industrial powers, along with the United States, Japan, and Germany. However, France has limited mineral resources. Most of the iron ore needed for steel has to be bought abroad. Cars and airplanes are major exports, along with plastics and chemicals. Perfumes and fashion goods are also sold abroad. With little coal and natural gas, France makes most of its electricity from nuclear power. The nuclear reactors use uranium that is mined in the Massif Central.

△ **Children carrying French bread**
The traditional French loaf is a long stick of white bread covered in crust.

Farming

Large quantities of wheat, wine, and cheese are sold abroad. Wheat is grown in the northern regions. Plums and apricots grow farther south. Grape vineyards are found over much of the country. So, too, are cattle. Milk from sheep and goats is used in making cheeses.

Fishing

Most fishing takes place off the Atlantic coast. Today, there are fewer fish to catch in the Mediterranean. La Rochelle, located in the northwest, and Boulogne, on the north coast, are among the biggest fishing ports. Fish and shellfish play an important part in French cooking.

Food

French people take great pride in their food and how they prepare it. The word *cuisine*, which means "style of cooking," is a French word. French cuisine is among the best in the world. Here are a few popular dishes:

bouillabaisse: a fish stew made with small crabs, rockfish, crayfish, and other shellfish, seasoned with rosemary and saffron

mousse: a chilled dessert made with sweetened whipped cream or beaten egg whites and gelatin

ratatouille: a stew made with squash, green peppers, eggplant, tomatoes, and sometimes meat

vichyssoise: a cold soup made of pureed leeks or onions, potatoes, cream, and chicken stock

Schools

Children between the ages of two and six can go to nursery school. After six, all children must attend school until age sixteen. Some students continue their education at a lycée (high school) to study for the examination called the *baccalauréat*. Others attend a technical college to train for a career.

For older students, there are many universities to choose from. Since higher education is funded by the state, tuition fees are low.

The Media

Three out of five French men and women read a newspaper every day. They have a choice of about eighty daily national and regional newspapers. Some, such as *Le Monde* (The World) and *Le Figaro*, are world famous.

The magazines *Paris-Match*, *Elle*, and *Marie Claire* are well known and widely read outside France.

There are six main television channels to choose from, plus many others that are relayed by cable or satellite. There are also commercial radio stations.

△ **One of the "rose windows" in Chartres**
The cathedral has the finest medieval stained-glass windows in the world.

Drama

In the 18th century, Louis XIV, who was known as the Sun King, built the magnificent theater Comédie Française in Paris. He did so to honor the memory of the playwright Molière. Great French playwrights of modern times include Jean Anouilh, Jean Genet, and Eugène Ionesco.

Art

Art is part of the French way of life. When William of Normandy conquered England in 1066, his queen recorded the events in a beautiful tapestry. There are many examples of French art throughout the ages. These include magnificent cathedrals, such as the one at Chartres and Notre Dame in Paris, the paintings by such great artists as Paul Cézanne, Claude Monet, and Henri Matisse, and the movies made by Jean Renoir and other French directors. French fashion designers, such as Yves Saint Laurent, are world famous.

Literature

Several of the world's greatest writers were French. Some, such as René Descartes, François Voltaire, and Jean-Paul Sartre, were also great philosophers. Novelists like Victor Hugo, Honoré de Balzac, and Emile Zola also exposed the bad behavior of their times. Great French poets include Jean de La Fontaine, Charles Baudelaire, and Arthur Rimbaud, to name a few.

FRANCE FACTS AND FIGURES

Religion

There is no official religion for the country of France. However, French people are traditionally Christians, and most of them are Roman Catholics. Only two out of 100 are Protestants. There are also numbers of French Jews, as well as Muslims and members of other religions. Most French Muslims came from North Africa. In country villages, most people attend a Catholic mass service.

Sports

The French are a great sporting nation. They watch or play all kinds of individual and team sports. French soccer and rugby teams are noted for the style and flair with which they play.

Many major sporting events are held in France. Among these are the Tour de France, the world's toughest bicycle race, the French Open international tennis tournament, and the famous Prix de l'Arc de Triomphe horserace. Skiing and other winter sports also have a large following. France has long coastlines and water sports are enjoyed as much by the French as by their many visitors.

Tour de France The cyclists sprint down the Champs Elysées in Paris in the final stage of the world's greatest bicycle race.

Festivals

There are French festivals for the arts, music, and drama, as well as religious and historic festivals. Here is a small selection:

Mid to late May **Cannes Film Festival** Movie makers from all over the world come to this Mediterranean resort to promote their new films.

July 14 **Bastille Day** A national holiday that comemmorates the fall of the Bastille in Paris in 1789 and the beginning of the French Revolution.

Late November **"Les Trois Glorieuses"** The Burgundy region's biggest wine festival.

Plants

Oak forests grow in parts of northern and western France. Grains have been planted in much of the northeast. The Pyrenees and Massif Central have forests on their western and central slopes. In the southeast, olives, thyme, and rosemary are found along with hyacinths, tulips, orchids, and other wild flowers. The *maquis* — scrubland of trees and shrubs up to 6 feet (2 meters) high — covers the drier regions of France and much of Corsica.

Animals

Wild boar live in forests not far from Paris. The Pyrenees and the Alps are home to Chamois deer and the Spanish goat. Brown bears, which are now rare in Europe, are also believed to still live in the Pyrenees. The Camargue, in the Rhône Delta, has wild horses, bulls, and flamingos. Numerous insects and reptiles, including snakes, lizards, and tortoises are found in the south. The rivers and lakes are full of trout, pike, and perch. Coastal waters contain a wide variety of fish and shellfish.

HISTORY

People lived in France as long as 20,000 years ago. Celts from the east arrived about 500 B.C. From the middle of the 1st century B.C. the country was under Roman rule. The Romans called the land Gaul. As Roman rule weakened, various peoples arrived and fought each other for land. The most successful of these peoples were the Franks. The Frankish empire reached its height in the 8th century under the king Charlemagne.

Afterward, the empire broke up. France lost land to England, but gradually won it back in a series of wars between 1337 and 1453. In 1789, the monarchy was overthrown by the French Revolution. This led to wars between France and most of its neighbors. In 1804, Napoleon Bonaparte became emperor of France. But he was sent into exile after defeat at the Battle of Waterloo in 1815. A second revolution in 1848 ended the French monarchy forever.

During the 19th century, France seized colonies in North Africa and Southeast Asia. There was heavy fighting on French soil in both World War I (1914–1918) and World War II (1939–1945). Starting in June 1944, U.S., British, and other troops, aided by members of the French resistance, won back France from the Germans. After World War II, under President Charles de Gaulle, France granted independence to its colonies. France and its old enemy Germany became founding members of the European Community. French presidential elections are held every five years.

LANGUAGE

French grew out of Latin, the language of the Romans. The people who lived in France at the time of the Roman invasion adopted the language of their conquerors. But they also added some Celtic and Germanic words. For centuries, French was widely spoken by educated people throughout Europe. Today, it is still one of the world's most important languages. Although in some regions of the country other languages are spoken, French is the common language.

Useful words and phrases

English	French
Zero	zéro
One	un, une
Two	deux
Three	trois
Four	quatre
Five	cinq
Six	six
Seven	sept
Eight	huit
Nine	neuf
Ten	dix
Sunday	dimanche
Monday	lundi
Tuesday	mardi

Useful words and phrases

Wednesday	mercredi
Thursday	jeudi
Friday	vendredi
Saturday	samedi
Good morning	Bonjour
Good evening	Bonsoir
Good night	Bonne nuit
Good-bye	Au revoir
Please	S'il vous plaît
Thank you	Merci
How are you?	Comment allez-vous?
Very well, thank you	Très bien, merci
Excuse me	Excusez-moi

INDEX

Book created for Highlights for Children, Inc. by Bender Richardson White.
Editors and make-up: Peter MacDonald and Lionel Bender
Designer: Malcolm Smythe
Art Editor: Ben White
Editorial Assistant: Madeleine Samuel
Picture Researcher: Madeleine Samuel
Production: Kim Richardson

Maps produced by Oxford Cartographers, England.
Currency from MRI Bankers Guide to Foreign Currency.
Stamps courtesy of Scott Publishing Co., Sidney, OH 45365 (www.scottonline.com).

Editorial Consultant: Andrew Gutelle.
Guide to France was produced with the help of the French Tourist Office, London.
French Consultants: Michel Duplaix and Anne Duplaix, Neuilly, France.
Managing Editor, Highlights New Products: Margie Hayes Richmond

Picture credits
DS = David Simson/ DAS Photographs. EU = Eye Ubiquitous. Z = Zefa.
t = top, b = bottom, l = left, r = right.

Cover: Z/Weir. Pages: 6l: DS. 6-7: Z/Weir. 7: X. 8t: DS. 8b: EU/Paul Seheult. 9: DS. 10: DS. 11t: DS. 11b: Z. 12-13: EU/James Davis Travel Photography. 13t: DS. 13b: Z. 14l: Lionheart Books. 15t: DS. 15b: DS. 16, 17t, 17b: Z. 18: Z/Kerth. 19t: EU/Chris Bland. 19b: Z/Starfoto. 20: Z/Strange. 21l: Z. 21r: EU/Selby. 22: EU/Darren C. Maybury. 23t: Lionheart Books. 23b: DS. 24: EU/Peter Palmer. 25t: Z. Dr. H Wirth. 25b: Z. 26: EU/Tim Hawkins 26-27: Z/Hackman. 27t: DS. 28: DS. 29: Z/Eugen. 30: EU/B. Harding.
Illustration on Page 1 by Tom Powers